Being Intimate

Achieving Union With Others Without Losing Yourself

Dale R. Olen, Ph.D.

A Life Skills Series Book

JODA Communications, Ltd.
Milwaukee, Wisconsin

Editor: Carolyn Kott Washburne
Design: Chris Roerden and Associates
Layout: Eileen Olen

ISBN 1-56583-008-3

Published by: JODA Communications, Ltd.
                10125 West North Avenue
                Milwaukee, WI 53226

PRINTED IN THE UNITED STATES OF AMERICA

"Pot Shots" reprinted by permission of
Ashleigh Brilliant, copyright © 1980.

Table of Contents

Introduction

to the
Life Skills Series

Nobody gets out alive! It isn't easy navigating your way through life. Your relationships, parents, marriage, children, job, school, church, all make big demands on you. Sometimes you feel rather ill-equipped to make this journey. You feel as if you have been tossed out in the cold without even a warm jacket. Life's journey demands considerable skill. Navigating the sometimes smooth, other times treacherous journey calls for a wide variety of tools and talents. When the ride feels like a sailboat pushed by a gentle breeze, slicing through the still waters, you go with the flow. You live naturally with the skills already developed.

But other times (and these other times can make you forget the smooth sailing), the sea turns. The boat shifts violently, driven by the waves' force. At those stormy moments, you look at your personal resources, and they just don't seem sufficient.

Gabriel Marcel, the French philosopher, wrote that the journey of life is like a spiral. The Greeks, he observed, viewed life as *cyclical*–sort of the same old thing over and over. The seasons came, went, and came again. History repeated itself. The Hebrews, on the other hand, saw life as *linear*–a pretty straight march toward a goal. You begin at the Alpha point and end at Omega. It's as simple as that.

Marcel combined the two views by capturing the goal-oriented optimism of the Hebrews and the sobering reality of the Greeks' cycles. Life has its ups and downs, but it always moves forward.

To minimize the *downs* and to make the most of the *ups*, you need **Life Skills**. When you hike down the Grand Canyon, you use particular muscles in your back and legs. And when you trudge up the Canyon, you use other muscles. So too with life skills. You call on certain skills when your life spirals down, such as the skill of defeating depression and managing stress. When your life is on an upswing, you employ skills like thinking reasonably and meeting life head on.

This series of books is about the skills you need for getting through life. To get from beginning to end without falling flat on your face and to achieve some dignity and some self-satisfaction, you need **basic** life skills. These include:

1. Accepting yourself.
2. Thinking reasonably.
3. Meeting life head on.

With these three life skills mastered to some degree, you can get a handle on your life. Now, if you want to build from there, you are going to need a few more skills. These include:

4. Communicating.
5. Managing stress.
6. Being intimate.
7. Resolving conflict.
8. Reducing anger.
9. Overcoming fear.
10. Defeating depression.

If you have these ten skills up and running in your life, you are ready to face yourself, your relationships, your parents, your marriage, your children, your job and even God with the hope of handling whatever comes your way. Without these skills, you are going to bump into one stone wall after another. These skills don't take away the problems, the challenges and the hard times. But they do help you dig out of life's deep trenches and more fully *enjoy* the good times.

Life Skills can be learned. You have what it takes to master each of these skills–even if you feel you don't have the tiniest bit of the skill right now. But nobody can develop the skill for you. You have to take charge and develop it yourself. Your family, friends and community may be able to help you, but you are the center at which each skill has to start. Here is all you need to begin this learning process:

- Awareness.
- The desire to grow.
- Effort and practice.

Awareness begins the process of change. You have to notice yourself, watch your behavior and honestly face your strengths and weaknesses. You have to take stock of each skill and of the obstacles in you that might inhibit its growth.

Once you recognize the value of a skill and focus on it, you have to want to pursue it. The critical principle here, one you will see throughout this series, is *desire*. Your desire will force you to focus on the growing you want to do and keep you going when learning comes hard.

Finally, your *effort and practice* will make these **Life Skills** come alive for you. You can do it. The ten books in the **Life Skills Series** are tools to guide and encourage your progress. They are my way of being with you–cheering your efforts. But without your practice, what you find in these books will wash out to sea.

Working on these ten **Life Skills** won't get you through life without any scars. But the effort you put in will help you measure your life in more than years. Your life will be measured in the zest, faith, love, honesty and generosity you bring to yourself and your relationships.

I can hardly wait for you to get started!

Chapter One

What is the Skill of Being Intimate?

T he mental hospital had been their home for the past 12 years. Both had been diagnosed paranoid schizophrenic. When they first came to St. Joseph's, George and Henry felt safest in their fantasy world of hallucinations and delusions. As time went on, and the medication and treatment took effect, the fantasy world gave way to the real world.

In that real world these two men became friends. They enjoyed each other's company. They played cards together, went on walks and watched the same programs on television. Occasionally, one of the men relapsed into his fantasy world. He was no longer George. Instead he became a horse. He would get down on all fours, prance around the hospital wing and look to eat grass. His friend, Henry, would become distraught. He couldn't stand to lose his friend. George was his buddy, not this horse! He couldn't connect to a horse. A horse couldn't play cards or watch television, although he could, perhaps, go for a walk.

At times like this, Henry desperately wanted to connect to

George. But how? Eventually he discovered the way. One morning an orderly observed George grazing around the television room, apparently looking for hay. Slightly behind him, also on all fours, barked Henry. When Henry barked, George jumped and ran forward. Pretty soon the two of them were walking through the hallways, George neighing to Henry, Henry barking to George. Once again, they were connected.

Henry so needed to remain connected to George, he bought into George's delusion of being a horse by becoming a dog. He actually left his own reality to enter a fantasy world with his dear friend. To paraphrase a line from the Bible: "Greater love than this no man has than to go crazy in order to be with his friend."

The drive toward intimacy, toward closeness with another, weaves its way through every dynamic of your life. It stands as your most fundamental energy. From infancy you have focused on one agenda – to be connected.

Remember Gabriel Marcel from the Introduction to this book? He saw life as a spiral. He also made a profound comment about intimacy and being connected. He said the first proof that you exist (if you need to prove it to yourself) lies in this realization: *"We are, therefore I am."* In other words, because you're connected to someone, you know you exist. But you want more than simple existence and connection. You want intimacy. You want to be close to someone.

So, what is intimacy and how do you get it?

Maybe it happened when you were 19. You met after a basketball game. You liked each other, you could tell. You talked that night for hours. You realized the conversation must have been going on for a long time, because wasn't that the sun coming up? It felt so easy. You seemed to fit so well with each other. The words simply flowed, the topics wove in and out, covering everything from capital punishment to your immature brothers. You were good with each other.

That night you shared more deeply than you ever had before. You felt like someone really knew you. You entered into the exciting world of another's life. You were close after one night. Poems are written of such intimacy.

The next day you called early, talked briefly, but craved to continue the conversation. You met for lunch, skipped your afternoon classes and walked the campus, sharing more and more. You found yourselves holding hands. It seemed so natural. By evening you kissed and held each other. The night must never end. For now, you felt, the two of you were one. Two "I's" became a "we."

You attained some kind of intimacy in 24 hours. You shared with each other your innermost thoughts and feelings as best you could. Of course, with only 19 years under your belt, you had only so many thoughts and feelings. But what you had you shared. Intimacy, for you at 19, meant talking about everything, listening intently, hugging and kissing before sadly saying goodnight.

Forty years later, you still talk, but not as much, perhaps, and certainly not into the early morning hours. You get to bed by 10:30. You give each other a light kiss, and you're sound asleep in minutes. You do the grocery shopping together and watch a movie video on Friday evening. You take nice vacations, where you *feel* close again. You know you're intimate, but on vacations you feel it.

When a grandchild cries and your daughter gets upset with her, you glance at your husband or wife, smile ever so slightly and wink. No words, but you both remember when that daughter of yours was a tiny, crying child. Intimacy? Absolutely. More so than when you were 19? Absolutely. Now, you have forty additional years of experience, but this time *together*. Living your lives together all these years creates your intimacy. You have become so familiar to each other, you know exactly what the other is thinking, feeling and about to do. Your intimacy comes from shared experience, shared joys and sorrows, shared thoughts. It comes from walking the path of life together, you and your partner.

Here, then, are the characteristics of intimacy.

Intimacy involves sharing yourself and your possessions with another in a mutual way.

Sharing, of course, stands as the basis of intimacy. It's how intimacy happens. *Mutuality* is the other important word here. The sharing must be mutual. Psychotherapy involves a lot of deep sharing, but it goes only in one direction, from the client to the therapist. In an intimate relationship, it must go both ways.

Sharing possessions as well as thoughts and feelings increases intimacy. The "What's mine is yours" mentality works much better in marriages than a "Let's keep track of what's mine and what's yours" way of thinking. In truly intimate relationships, all your "stuff" becomes the "stuff" of the other as well.

Intimacy involves mutual understanding with the loved one.

The only way you can get "mutual sharing" to occur is through *mutual understanding*. Sharing includes giving *and* receiving. The better you are at sensitively understanding the other, the more sharing of self the other will do.

Often at the beginning of a relationship such understanding comes easily. You're anxious to know who that creature is. You listen closely. You attend fully, no distractions. You actually feel as though you can enter the experience of the other. As the years go by and the novelty of the other's world wears off, you can easily lose attention. You can get distracted while the other talks on and on. You used to like all that conversation, but now it seems so repetitious. You've heard it all before, you think.

Listening opens up the sharing experience. It makes the other feel safe when revealing. It allows the other freedom to share at whatever level feels comfortable. It's the skill most needed to develop the experience of intimacy.

Intimacy encourages the positive interpretation of the other's motives.

A terrible thing happens when you don't like someone else. You interpret his or her motives in a negative way. When you view another person as against you, you assign sinister motives to that person's behavior. You say, "The reason he made that comment in the meeting is because he wants to show me up." Or in a more intimate setting, "She never listens to my point of view. She is so self-centered."

When you feel close to another, you interpret his behavior in a positive way. You know he loves you, so when he acts otherwise, you conclude it was simply an oversight on his part. He merely forgot to call the restaurant for reservations as you asked him to do.

Positive interpretations of the other's behavior are the sure sign of intimacy in a relationship. Giving the other the benefit of the doubt and casting that person in an affirming light signals the closeness and confidence of the relationship. Negative interpretations are the sand particles in the gears of a relationship that grind it to an ugly halt.

Intimacy means holding the loved one in high regard.

You just bought a brand new car, a sparkling, red, sporty number, cut low to the ground. You take care of that new car the way close friends take care of each other. You value it. You guard it, parking it at the far end of lots so it gets no pings. You wash and wax it and follow the maintenance schedule regularly.

You show your car off. You're proud to be seen tooling around the neighborhood. You defend your car when it gets compared to other makes and models. Now, I don't want to carry this analogy too far, but the sense of regard that goes into owning a new car, buying a new house or loving a special book also goes into forming an intimate relationship.

In such a relationship you value that other person. You treat her in a special way. You attend to her at gatherings. You remain conscious of her, knowing that no one here holds a candle to this wonderful person. She is special, and you're thrilled in knowing that you and she are partners.

Intimacy means promoting the good of the loved one.

It follows that if you value her, you then seek what is good for her. You attend to her needs and wishes. When you know them, you attempt to meet those needs. Your focus is on her. She stands at the center of your life. In the ideal intimate relationship, both of you center in the other's life. By doing so, you both find your own needs met and delight in responding to each other's needs. You get the best of both worlds.

You also encourage each other's growth. You call her beyond herself, supporting her efforts to become a full and graceful person. She may want to go back to school. You pitch in even more with the care of the children. You adjust your schedule to accommodate her. You cut back your activities so she can become involved in that special program for six weeks. Whatever it takes to help her develop her potential, you want to do.

Intimacy means you can depend on each other at all times.

Often with casual friends and neighbors, you hesitate to ask them for a favor. Your child needs to get picked up late from school, but you can't do it. You could ask your neighbor, but you don't want to impose. So you change your plans and get the child yourself. If you were in a more intimate relationship with your neighbor, you would not hesitate to ask. You would feel free because you know she will do it if she can. And if she can't, you know she will tell you that.

In an intimate marriage, all hesitation is lost. You feel perfectly comfortable asking your husband to get the mail, pick up the kids and take down the laundry. Why? Because in intimate relationships, you rely on each other. You view yourselves as partners, working together for your combined good.

In intimate marriages, for instance, couples realize that they are responsible *together*. If one is still working hard while the other relaxes with the paper and wine, then something's breaking down in this partnership. Intimate couples work with each other, although not always at the same tasks. Then they relax together, play together and rest together. They assist each other and send the message that the other can call for help anytime.

Intimacy is one aspect of a full loving relationship.

The best description I have seen of a full, loving relationship has been offered by Robert Sternberg in his book, *The Triangle of Love* (Basic Books, 1987). He describes three aspects necessary for love: passion, intimacy and commitment.

Briefly, *passion* is the draw. It's often the first element present. It brings two people together. They find themselves attracted to each other. Part of that draw can be sexual, but passion is more than sex. It calls the two to make contact, to spend time together, to know each other. Passion allows people to put the word "in" before the word "love." "Are you 'in love' with her?" "Well, I love her, but I don't know if I'm *in* love with her." You will be "in love" when you feel the strong draw, the passion for her.

Intimacy involves the mutual sharing of selves. It includes all those aspects described above. It's the friendship aspect of a full relationship. It contains warmth, positive feelings for the other and a desire to act for the other's well-being. I believe it's the most important of the three aspects of love. Intimacy must be maintained at a high level for passion and commitment to endure.

Commitment brings the triangle of love to completion. If you have passion and deep intimacy in a relationship, you will move gracefully toward commitment. This aspect comes from the rational power within you. It serves as a statement of fidelity and longevity. By your commitment you say, "I take you for better or worse. I will stand with you no matter what, even when I don't feel like it. I'm here for the long haul."

Intimacy leads to happiness. While it occasionally contains pain, worry and sadness, it will fill you up with delight and contentment. Knowing you walk through life with someone at your side makes the difficult times more bearable and magnifies the wonderful times immensely. Although you may hesitate at the door of intimacy, I hope you will courageously open that door and enter. As you enter I want you to carry the principles and tools of intimacy you are about to learn in the remainder of this book. By doing so you will discover the riches intimacy has to offer you.

Chapter Two

Principles and Tools for Being Intimate

Principle 1

Try to move toward people rather than away from them.

Most likely you agree with this statement. The majority of people do. Yet very few, I believe, live it out with ease in their daily lives. It's hard to routinely move toward others. Oftentimes, you'll tend to withdraw and back away from people. Many child psychologists point out that children deal with interpersonal conflict by withdrawal and denial. So do we as adults.

Actually, whether you move toward or away from another person is determined by your level of *comfort* with intimacy in relationships. When you reach your point of comfort, you tend to stop moving toward or away from others. You like it right where you are. That feels just right, sort of like the baby pig in the Three Little Pigs story.

Your personal *comfort* determines the level of intimacy you reach in your relationships. If too much intimacy causes anxiety, stress or pain, then you back up from the other. On the other hand, if you find contentment and nurturance in a very close relationship, you continue moving toward the other in more intimate ways.

So, you do one of two things based on your comfort with intimacy: First, you may seek a high degree of closeness because you enjoy it. You feel content with it. It fulfills you. Or, second, you prefer a certain distance. You feel better when your relationship has clear, tight boundaries with plenty of space between the two of you. You like it when there is sufficient distance between you and the other. You feel safe knowing you can always back up when necessary.

You and your partner both bring your histories and beliefs about intimacy into your relationship. What if you feel very comfortable with a high degree of intimacy, but your partner prefers distance? What happens if you move toward him to feel closer, and he backs away because that much closeness makes him feel uncomfortable? Usually, the one who wants more intimacy feels frustrated and unfulfilled. The one who wants distance feels pressured and criticized. *If you and your partner are not comfortable with the same degree of intimacy, conflict will tend to arise.*

You can understand this better if you imagine yourselves on your own personal Distance-Intimacy Continuum. If you fall close to the same positions on your continua, you should have a satisfying and fulfilling relationship. However, if you fall at different points on those continua, you will have major adjustments to make in order for both of you to find happiness in your relationship.

Let's draw it out so you can see what it looks like:

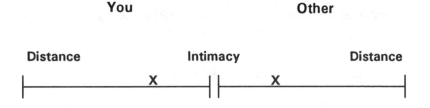

In this instance you and your partner would be compatible. You each want about the same level of intimacy. Your comfort levels match.

If your levels of comfort with intimacy were very different, your Distance-Intimacy Continua would look like this:

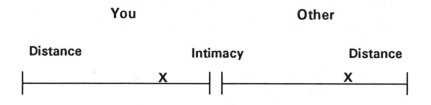

In this situation you would experience high levels of incompatibility. While you would seek more and more intimacy, your partner would back away from it. For instance, you might attempt to get closer to Tom by talking with him about your feelings of inadequacy at work. You share your anxiety, your discouragement and your disappointment in yourself. You want him to come close to you and comfort you. Without naming it as such, you're seeking deeper levels of intimacy.

But Tom, who finds such closeness uncomfortable, retreats as you come forward. After repeated attempts by you to reach Tom, you become discouraged and back up by getting quiet and doing some pouting. Tom senses your movement away. Because he is not comfortable with *too* much distance, he begins to move toward you by asking what's wrong and how you're feeling. When you detect his movement toward you and his new warmth, you begin, once again, to approach him. Of course, when you do that, Tom again feels the closeness creeping in, becomes anxious about it and backs up to his place of comfort.

So this "dance of intimacy" continues. If you come too close, he backs up. If you retreat too far, he moves toward you. You then re-approach him and he flees from you. Since he's more comfortable with a greater degree of distance and seeks less intimacy than you do, he always controls the amount of closeness in the relationship. Since you seek the deeper level of intimacy, you always experience a higher level of frustration and dissatisfaction in the relationship. Consequently, he also perceives you as the more active, the more complaining or nagging and the more anxious to get the relationship "fixed."

Personal comfort, then, usually controls the depth of your relationships. If you have been hurt in relationships and have fostered negative beliefs about closeness, you will stand back from deep intimacy. While understandable, the more helpful stance is to *move toward* others rather than away from them.

This is particularly true in special friendships and in marriage. Here intimacy serves as the essential glue that holds the relationship together. But this principle also works in casual friendships and in acquaintanceships as well. Moving toward the other in an interested, caring and assertive manner brings energy to a relationship. It creates "chemistry" that invigorates you and the other. You both leave the encounter feeling refreshed and "up."

Principle 2

**Develop clear personal boundaries between
you and the other person.**

Before birth, you had no boundaries. You were merged with Mother – body and spirit. You knew only *union*. You literally swam in an ocean of harmony, where no barriers existed. Then you were birthed – your first awesome experience of separateness. From then on, you have lived in ambivalence, longing at some primitive level to regain the intimate union you once knew, and at the same time struggling to live separate and free from others.

Throughout your childhood you struggled to set boundaries and define who you were. You tried separating from your mom and merging with your dad. Then you tried identifying and becoming one with your mom again and rejecting your dad. You fought with your older brother and felt close to your younger sister. You had a new best friend every other day or week. Then you had no best friends, but wanted only to be part of the gang. As a child, you tried out a lot of boundary-setting and boundary-breaking styles, trying to decide where you ended and the other began.

In your teen years you still did not possess clear boundaries. You invaded others' spaces. You weren't sure where you stopped and others began. You took your sister's clothes. You walked into your brother's room uninvited and borrowed his music tapes. You left your towel on the bathroom floor and didn't clean the junk off the car seat after using it. At the same time, you said "no" easily and frequently. You tried hard to separate from those who had taught you union. You argued with Mom and announced your desire to have a different parent. You stayed out past curfew and refused to go to church with the family.

Your task during adolescence was to put boundaries in your life. You wanted to be separate from but at the same time united with your parents and family. If you didn't learn to set clear boundaries between yourself and others then, you're paying the price now in your adult relationships. You are most likely living enmeshed in the life of your partner.

To be enmeshed means living in the other person's "space" rather than your own. Physically, that's easy to see. When a husband strikes his wife in anger, or when a man pushes himself onto a woman sexually, he invades her space. He lives in her world. However, if she invites him in and he enters, enmeshment at the physical level, at least, is not taking place.

Psychological and emotional enmeshment is more difficult to see, but much more common. Here you don't simply "invade" the other's space. Rather, you *identify* with the other. You define who you are based on your relationship with the other person. If that person changes, so do you. You see your worth according to the other's responses: "If she loves me and showers me with affection, then I am worth something. If she stops and becomes angry with me, then I am nothing."

Enmeshment also occurs when you *project* onto the other. Projection simply means denying some aspect of yourself and putting it onto the other person. You keep the good qualities and push the not-so-good onto your partner. Anger, jealousy, a sense of inadequacy and fear are some qualities you can easily project onto your partner. You get angry. But because you have been taught never to show anger, you deny it and see anger in your partner. You might be afraid of intimacy, yet want it. So you keep your distance from your friend but blame him for not being close to you. Most projections are not conscious and are difficult to get in touch with.

Sometimes projections can be positive. If you like a particular characteristic about yourself, you will see it in others, even when it might not be there. You see yourself as outgoing and friendly. You relate to a man who is actually somewhat reserved. But because you so want an outgoing kind of life, you view him as much more outgoing than he actually is. Such an approach, of course, can cause difficulty at some point, usually when you can finally admit how reserved he is.

What is needed in all relationships is *clear boundaries*. You need to understand and accept yourself in order to effectively interact at any deep level. Boundaries allow you clarity. They help you define yourself, so you know what it is you are giving in a relationship. To develop these clear boundaries you need ever increasing levels of personal awareness.

If you don't have distinct boundaries, you will often focus on others. You will not attend to yourself, to what you are thinking, feeling, experiencing. You will live outside of yourself, usually in other people's territory. To gain a sense of self, living within your own space, you need to become much more aware of and accepting of yourself, independently of others. That means you need to take time alone. In that time you need to become aware of your thoughts, urges, desires, feelings, values and beliefs. Then you need to say, "What I believe and feel is part of *me*. It is different and distinct from what others think and feel. What they think is fine for them. What I experience is fine for me."

Your boundaries also become clearer for you when you understand the limitations of your own power. When you are enmeshed, you attempt to control the other. You take responsibility for the actions and decisions of the other. But, when your boundaries are clear, you realize you do not have that kind of power in other people's lives. You don't take responsibility for their actions. For instance, you know you can't make her stop smoking. You can't control his workaholic life style. You can't force your teenager to talk with you. When you know your boundaries, you also know the limitations of your power.

With clear boundaries, you learn to feel with others, involve yourself with others, but also accept the other's independence. You realize that others make their own choices and must accept the consequences of those choices. You will cross your own boundaries and enter the other's space only upon request, and you will do so gently and with respect.

Principle 3

**Create positive labels to allow the relationship
to grow more fully.**

Any time you label something two things happen: one, it helps you understand the object; and two, it limits your further perception and often controls the object from changing. Naming something lets you gain a better sense of it. You see an object in the sand. You can't tell if it's alive or inanimate. You study it and finally conclude it's simply a stone. Once you label it, you put it in a category or a stereotype. "Oh yes," you think, "my understanding of the group of things we call stones is that they are harmless objects as long as they are left alone. They can be beautiful to look at. And they can be fun to play with around lakes and oceans." You have labeled and stereotyped the stone. Now you are ready to react to it. In this case you pick it up and skip it out into the ocean because that's how you have fun with stones.

The same occurs with people. After spending some time with a person in therapy, I may place a label on him or her. In psychology, we diagnose the person and put her in a category or stereotype. I call her an obsessive-compulsive individual. That label helps me understand certain dynamics about her. She tends to think in perfectionistic ways. She seeks certainty. She experiences guilt, and so on. If I am accurate in my labeling of her, then the label helps me know her better.

But labels and stereotypes also limit your understanding and often control the behavior of the other. Once you label something one way, it becomes increasingly difficult to view it another way. Once you decide, based on your view, that opera is unintelligible to English-speaking people, you won't want to attend a "new and exciting opera" at the Arts Center.

So, for example, you may label your cousin a "know-it-all." Once you do that, you color everything he says by adding, "Oh, he thinks he knows it all anyway." You may conclude, "There's no point giving him my opinion." So based on your label, you no longer listen attentively to him, and you don't communicate anything to him. Your lack of conversation leaves a void between you, which he fills by telling you more and more about all he knows. In other words, your label or stereotype of him becomes a self-fulfilling prophecy.

Some of our most powerful labeling occurs around sex roles.

Many of these stereotypes you learned as a child and had reinforced by the media and other cultural forces. I became dramatically aware of this when my son was five and my daughter three. My wife and I had made a deliberate effort to avoid using sexist language with our children. So one day Andy said to me, "Dad, when I grow up I'm going to be a fireman."

I said, "That's nice, Andy. But you will be a fire *person*."

He responded, "Oh no, I'm going to be a fire*man*. Women can't be firemen."

Said I, the teacher, "Oh, yes they can. And they can do it very well."

He thought for a moment. Then I saw the light go on in his mind. I sensed I had made my point. But he replied, "I guess girls can be firemen. When the fire alarm goes off, all the men will slide down the pole, jump on the trucks and go put out the fire. Then when they are done, they will drive back to the station, and the fire ladies will have supper ready for them." So much for raising a feminist son!

Common stereotypes of men include such descriptions as active, aggressive, logical and cool. Women are often seen as social, intuitive, emotional and sensitive. The man is self-reliant; the woman cares for people. If someone doesn't fit the stereotype, you then place another label on him or her in order to handle the discrepancy. You might call an emotional man a "wimp" or an assertive woman a "nag." Once you place the label on someone, it becomes increasingly difficult for that person to get free from its shackles.

On the other hand, if you give the other person a positive label, he or she tends to thrive under it. Generally, when a relationship is working well, you view the other in positive terms. (Of course, using positive labels for one another strengthens the relationship as well.) If you see your partner as "sensitive," then when she acts insensitively toward you, you dismiss it and blame a force outside of her. You say, "It's been a long day for her. She is just tired." She remains a sensitive and good person in your eyes.

But if the relationship is breaking down, it may be due to negative labeling. "He is a selfish person," you think. Then when he does an unselfish deed for you (such as volunteers to pick up the kids), you interpret that as caused by something outside of himself. You figure, "He's just setting me up to ask for something. Otherwise he wouldn't have volunteered." Labels control your vision and often the behavior of the other.

If you must label or stereotype the other, then create positive labels. This allows you to keep seeing the other in an optimistic light and give the other room to make changes. With such changes, the other can move closer to you.

To create positive labels:

1. Pay close attention to the various labels you have of your friend or partner. If any labels appear negative or limiting, attempt to challenge them and make them more positive.

2. Ask your partner if he or she feels controlled by your expectations or demands. His or her answer will give a good indication of possible hidden labels you have.

3. Try creating positive labels that are freeing. Write them down. "I see her as kind, gentle, quick to heal any division, a sports' fan, intelligent, an achiever, a good mother, a career woman, a feminist, independent, and so on."

Principle 4

Keep the other person a top priority.

At the beginning of a close relationship, you become preoccupied with thoughts about the other. He intrudes into your daily life. You wonder what he's doing, when you will see him next and so on. He becomes the center of your attention.

As the relationship develops, you keep your focus on him. As you come to know him, you recognize what pleases and dissatisfies him, what he needs and doesn't need, what he values and objects to. Based on these awarenesses you respond to him accordingly. You think to ask about the meeting he ran, the headache he complained about this morning, the book report project. You remember how much he likes ice cream, and you pick some up. You know he enjoys classical music, and you buy him a compact disc just for the heck of it.

Now, if this sensitivity and other-centeredness could only continue! For some people it does. But for the majority, things gradually change. As your relationship progresses, you tend to lose some of the intense focus on the other. Gradually, you return to attending to your own needs, becoming again more sensitive to your own center rather than to your partner's. This response is normal and doesn't mean you love the other less.

You have always been the center of your own life. No one else can be your center, nor you another's center, indefinitely. So naturally you return to your home base, sensing your own desires, wishes and needs. As you shift your attention from the other to yourself, she may feel the change. Of course, she liked it better the other way. This shift can cause tension in the relationship.

What also occurs as you refocus on yourself is a tendency to "go off" in the other's presence. By this I mean you relax your attention toward the other and simply let down. When you were first getting to know each other, you were both on your best behavior – courteous, polite, attentive, alert to each other's needs. As time went on, you realized how much energy it took to be "on" for your friend – in addition to being "on" at work and in public, responding to others and adapting to your surroundings.

In your private life you like to turn off the switch. At home you don't need to impress anyone, you don't have to watch what you say or do, and you don't have to play the social games. In your off time you can simply be. Once a special relationship reaches a stable period, you feel the other person is part of your "off-time" life. Around this person, you think, you can be yourself. Unfortunately, being off tends to mean you become a little more self-centered, interested in your own refreshing activities. In off time you pull in your other-centered antennae as a way of caring for yourself and cutting off any further demands on your time.

At this point in the relationship you need to make an adjustment. If the relationship is important to you, then you need to re-center on the other person. Although you have brought the other into your "off-time" life because you like her so much, doing so contains the danger of ignoring her.

On the other hand, it may take too much psychic energy to keep her the center of your life indefinitely. A balance is needed. You can continue to make her the center of your attention when she's present and at certain other times. By doing so, you continue to strengthen the relationship. If both of you center on each other, you will discover, somewhat paradoxically, you can be "off" in the presence of one another, because your needs are being cared for. The longer you relate, centered on each other, the more likely you become part of each other's off time.

Principle 5

Work to love the *real* other and not the *ideal* other.

When you marry, four people enter the relationship. There is the *real* you and the *real* other; then there is the *idealized* you and the *idealized* other. When you enter a deep relationship, you have an image of how the other is to be. This image stems from your life experience. A woman told me her husband was just not very sensitive to her. He claimed he was sensitive and then cited twelve examples of just how sensitive he was. But her ideal of sensitivity was her father, who she claimed was "the most perfect man I have ever met." So, of course, her husband had to live up to that level of perfection. He couldn't do it. That upset the woman because she had anticipated marrying a man who would respond to her as her father responded to her mother.

The distance you experience between the ideal of your partner and his reality determines your satisfaction in the relationship. When a large gap exists between the real person and your idealization of

wide gap — IDEAL PARTNER / leads to / REAL PARTNER — great dissatisfaction

him, then you feel very dissatisfied with the relationship. Your partner never measures up. On the other hand, when your real partner comes close to your image of the ideal partner, you feel very satisfied in your relationship.

small gap — IDEAL PARTNER / leads to / REAL PARTNER — great satisfaction

When the gap between the ideal and real feels like the Grand Canyon, you have to work hard to shorten the distance between the two. Your first effort is to urge your partner to move up toward the ideal. If you just talk with him, you think, he will change and measure up to your ideal. Sometimes that works, but not always.

Next, you put some pressure on. You get under his real self and begin pushing upward, trying to get him to match the ideal you have of him. He may claim you're nagging and demanding. But you know you're just trying to get him to meet your ideal image. You'll be happy once he gets there.

When the slight pressure doesn't work, then you roll out the big guns. You bring in your anger. Anger serves as a lever to shove up the real to meet the ideal. Of course, this doesn't work well, because it pushes the other person away. He doesn't want to get close to a raging bull. Unfortunately for you, his reality now appears further from your ideal than ever before.

The other way of managing the gap between ideal and real is to understand just what you are doing. You're comparing this person to a fictional character. He can't live up to that. So you need to modify the ideal rather than force the real. Unfortunately, most people don't work this way. They keep attempting to change the reality to match the ideal. In fact, you live with greater peace of mind when you're willing to let go of your ideal partner and come to accept your real partner.

Principle 6

Accept the other for better and for worse.

I tell married couples frequently, "When you said 'I take you for better or for worse,' you never meant it." It takes time, intimacy and commitment to fully accept the other as she is. At the beginning of a marriage you say the words "for better or for worse," but you really believe, "In this relationship, there won't be any 'for worses.' Either she's so wonderful, she has no limitations. Or if there are limitations, I should be able to change her in a short period of time."

As the relationship goes on, you slowly realize that she does have some weak spots. There are dark corners that don't seem to change. At that point the words you said at the altar hit home. "I said I'd take her for better or for worse. Now is the moment of reckoning. Am I going to force her to change, so there are no 'for worses'? Or am I going to accept her with her dark side and love her all the same?"

In relationships that work the partners resolve this issue by accepting the darkness rather than by forcing change in the other. Psychologists refer to this effort as "the project of ambivalence." This is a life task that every one of us must engage. You need to work through this project in your own life first. Then you can accomplish it in your intimate relationships. You need to accept yourself for better *and* for worse. By facing, understanding and accepting your own dark side – or "shadow" as Carl Jung called it – you manage this important life task. When you accept your strengths and weaknesses, you come to inner peace. In the same respect when you learn to accept the pluses and minuses in your intimate partner, you also come to relational peace. The dynamic of force – attempting to create the other according to your image of perfection – gives way to understanding, acceptance and peace.

Principle 7

Develop an attitude of flexibility.

Once you accept your partner for better and for worse, you reach a high level of flexibility in your relationship. No question about this: relationships that work do so because both partners are flexible and spend time together. Those two qualities are found in all successful intimate relationships.

Rigid thinking and demanding attitudes have no place in intimate relationships. Such a mind-set imprisons both parties and kills the spontaneity necessary for a loving relationship. A rigid thinker makes demands on you, set rules for how you are to behave, and then enforces those rules. If you don't follow the rules, he sets them all the more strictly. He demands even more of you. He raises the ideal still higher, making it even more unrealistic for you to measure up. Rigid thinkers attempt to deal with the gap between the ideal and the real by heightening the ideal and then demanding that you, the real person, stretch even further to reach that ideal. Ultimately rigid thinkers destroy a relationship.

Al was an inflexible thinker who made many demands on his wife, Gloria. I asked him to write out as many of his absolute demands as he could think of. He compiled a list of 127. They ranged from "She should stay on her side of the bed," to "She should initiate sex at least half of the time." In between were such gems as:

"She should make my lunch even on her days off."

"She ought to keep the dirty dishes out of the sink."

"She shouldn't talk to me when I'm watching TV."

"She should come to bed at the same time I go to bed."

As you can imagine, this marriage had no chance for success as long as Al demanded Gloria's perfection.

So please work for flexibility. Accept the other as he or she is. Go with the flow of reality. You can continue to *wish* for the ideal to be reached. But you must still accept the real. You cannot *demand* that the other must be the way you want. Ashley Brilliant ©, a T-shirt philosopher, once said on one of his T-shirts, "Just because I accept you as you are does not mean I have abandoned my hope of your improving." You can *wish* that your partner changes, but you cannot *demand* that change. You need to accept him or her for better and for worse.

Just in case you're objecting to the notion of "acceptance at all costs," let me add: In certain instances you need to decide if you want to accept the limitations of the other. You may decide you cannot live with those limitations. You have certain "rules," and those cannot be broken. For instance, her continued abuse of alcohol may be intolerable. His physical attacks and anger most likely will not let you remain in the relationship. In cases like these you don't have to remain with the person. But you still need to accept the *reality* of that person – "This *is* the way she is right now. Period." However, you need to accept your own reality, too, which might be that you cannot live with someone who acts in this way. Then you need to leave the relationship.

In general, however, the more accepting and flexible you are in relation to one another, the more likely you will enjoy each other's company for a long time. If you spend time together, along with that flexibility, you will enjoy a highly successful relationship.

Principle 8

Be ready and willing to forgive and be forgiven.

When you are able to forgive and be forgiven, you can be sure you have mastered the "project of ambivalence." Only when you can say "I am sorry" and "I accept your apology," can you be sure you have faced your own limitations.

Clearly, you won't say you're sorry if you believe you have done no wrong. You also won't accept the apology of the other if you don't accept that she is limited and flawed. Yet that is your reality. You and the other possess strengths, but also weaknesses. When you face the weakness in yourself and the other, you can then say and mean those magical words: "I am sorry" and "I forgive you."

When you are hurt by the other, you need an apology to restore the balance in the relationship. If the apology does not come, you tend to hold on to the hurt and the anger that always accompanies hurt. You feel hurt when you focus on what you have lost; you feel anger when you focus on the one who made you lose something.

When you hurt, you want the other to know just how much he hurt you. You want him to feel some of your pain. By staying angry with him, you hope he experiences some of that hurt.

If he comes to you, grieving his offense, truly remorseful, then you can accept the apology and let go of your anger and hurt. If, on the other hand, his apology is absent or too casual, then it signals to you that he isn't hurting the way you are. In that case, you can't let go of your hurt and anger. You believe he must know your hurt by hurting for hurting you (if you follow that!).

You may also be unwilling to forgive if you don't see a change in the other's behavior. If your friend hurts you by failing to call when he says he will, then you won't forgive him if he continues to not call when he tells you he will. Forgiveness comes when the other's behavior changes along with his sorrow.

To forgive, then, means letting go of your ideal image of how the other is supposed to behave. Accept him as he is. Focus on his reality rather than your idealization of him. Then letting go becomes easier. Accept your own reality as well, knowing that you, too, make mistakes. You need his flexibility, understanding, acceptance and forgiveness as much as he needs yours.

Principle 9

**Understand that your emotional responses
decrease over time as your intimacy increases.**

A strange thing takes place in intimate relationships. The longer you know someone, the less emotion you feel with that person. You may think you are loving that person less. You may worry about the lack of intensity in the relationship. You may harken back to the "old days" when passion was high and love flooded your heart.

But you need not fear that you are drifting apart. In fact,

your lack of strong emotion may well be a sign of high intimacy. The more you know another, the more you can predict that person's responses. The more predictable the person is, the less surprise there is in the relationship. The less surprise, the less emotion you will feel.

When I first courted my wife, she lived in Chicago, I in Milwaukee. When I drove to Chicago to see her, my foot got heavier on the gas pedal and my heart beat faster the nearer to Chicago I came. I couldn't wait to see her. What would she be like today? What would she say? What would she be wearing? Would she still love me? I was always in for a surprise.

Now it's years later. I see Joelyn every day. We have shared so many joys and sorrows. We have reached deep levels of intimacy. We have talked and talked and talked. We know each other so well. Now when I drive home from work at night, my heart does not race. I drive the speed limit. She may not even be home when I arrive. Certainly I am glad to come home. But I know what to expect. I know how she will respond, what she will feel.

The more you know someone, the less emotion you feel, because you can predict that person's responses. It's helpful, however, to add emotion even to long-standing relationships. You can do that by bringing back the element of surprise. Break out of your routines. Bring spontaneity back into your life. Surprise creates emotion. Emotion tends to increase the passion in a relationship, which serves as the spice to give meaty intimacy its flavor.

Principle 10

To reach a deep level of intimacy, you need to reveal yourself through verbal communication.

You achieve union with another by opening up your inner life and allowing that person to see you and accept you as you are. You invite the other to know you fully, your strengths and limitations, your light and dark side, the obvious you and the secret you.

Words become your most effective tool in showing another person the varied and intriguing aspects of who you are. Words express thoughts, feelings, urges, impulses and intuitions more precisely than any other physical expression. While gestures, pantomimes, touches and vocal sounds all reveal the self, none seem to be as accurate or direct as words. The movement toward intimacy, then, grows on the strength of two people's ability to use words in order to express inner experiences.

An array of inner experiences can be shared verbally. The most simple involves narrating *events* of the *past* or *future* that don't personally involve you. World news, things that happened to the kids, gossip you overheard are all relatively easy to share.

Next, you can narrate *facts* about your own *past* or *future*. "I remember when I was 10, my dad took me to a baseball game." Talking about *present facts* brings you one step deeper in self-revelation: "I'm trying to finish up all this work before I watch television."

You take a major step in self-revealing when you share your *own opinions* and *beliefs* about *past* or *future events*. "I don't think we should make that trip next year." Sharing opinions about *present realities* sometimes takes a little more energy. "I think it would work better if we didn't yell at the kids so much."

You reach still further levels of self-revealing when you open up your *feelings* to one another. Telling your friend how you felt about a *past event* is perhaps the safest feeling to express. "I was very nervous before that meeting I had with the attorney a month ago." Expressing less comfortable feelings, such as resentment, sadness, anxiety, guilt, anger and so on, is generally more difficult than sharing feelings such as joy, peace, contentment or curiosity. Sharing the darker feelings like anger, hurt and worry tend to make you feel more vulnerable to the other person. Thus, you may resist sharing such feelings. But when you do, you achieve a very deep level of self-revelation, usually leading to greater acceptance and caring from the other person.

Sharing *feelings* about the *future* takes you even a step further in your efforts to self-reveal. What you feel about the future reveals something about you in the present. Actually, you *think* something about the future but experience the *feeling* in the present. "I really get excited when I think about going to Alaska." You are feeling something now and sharing it, but about a future event.

Finally, the deepest level of self-revelation occurs when you share *present feelings* about present events. At this point, you allow your friend to enter directly into your present experience. No longer are you sharing histories, but experience. Again, disclosing "darker" feelings in the present takes considerably more energy than sharing "lighter" feelings. "I am feeling sad right now because you didn't say anything about the award I got." Often, your deeper, more vulnerable feelings get covered by the one "dark" feeling most people can express with some ease – anger.

Anger masks vulnerability. It lays over hurt and pain. So you express it as a way of driving the other away and protecting yourself. Expressing anger can lead to deeper intimacy, but more frequently it drives a wedge into the relationship, causing separation rather than union.

Usually, other feelings lie beneath the anger, feelings that focus more on the self. Because anger directs your attention to the other, it seems easier to express. But if you honestly enter your present experience, you may find sadness, remorse, guilt, shame, hurt, worry, fear or jealousy beneath the anger. Expressing those emotions takes courage and a deep desire to gain closeness to the other.

Expressing warm and caring feelings in the present moment also signals a high level of self-revelation. Telling the other of your feelings of love, joy, contentment, tenderness and warmth does wonderful things in drawing two people closer together.

To become more verbally intimate:

1. Resolve to express verbally to the other whatever you experience. Ready yourself to pay attention to your thoughts and feelings and determine to express them through words.

2. Concentrate on the various ways of self-revealing and attempt to share at all levels, working from least to most revealing. You can share

> Facts: About non-personal things.
>
> About your own past or future.
>
> About your own present.
>
> Opinions and beliefs: About the past or future.
>
> About the present.
>
> Feelings: About the past.
>
> "light" *feelings.*
>
> "dark" *feelings.*
>
> About the future.
>
> About the present.
>
> vulnerable *feelings.*
>
> warm-caring *feelings.*

Principle 11

**The more you self-reveal,
the more the other person bonds to you.**

You shy away from opening yourself to others. You would rather remain distant. You wonder if the other will think less of you if he or she knows the *real* you.

What's going on? Either you believe that something *evil* lurks in your heart or you believe *nothing* is within. If you believe the first, then certainly you wouldn't want others to discover the evil. If you believe the second, then you become afraid the others will find out just how shallow and empty you are.

In fact, what happens is the opposite. When you reveal your inner life, others almost always respond positively. They see in you an inner goodness you don't recognize yourself. How can that be?

Imagine yourself talking to your friend, Sandy. In the conversation you tell her about your hateful feelings toward your brother, Tom. You pour out your soul to her, sharing how mean Tom was to you as a child and how he never supported you during your college years. Your feelings against him have grown stronger and you think you're an awful person for having such hateful feelings.

Sandy responds warmly to you. By the end of the conversation she's saying, "Thank you for sharing all of that. I never knew how you felt about him. This helps me understand you better. I feel much closer to you now than I did before." You can't understand her reaction. "How could she still like me after what I told her about myself?" you wonder.

But from her point of view, she noticed a fundamental inner goodness in you, a goodness you, yourself, could not see due to your early belief about being "bad". Even though you told her some unflattering things about your feelings, she still saw the goodness underneath. She noticed the deep passion you have to be loved and connected to your brother. She experienced your honesty and willingness to open yourself to her. She appreciated that you chose her to share with at such a personal level. She wants to know you even more.

When a person self-reveals, he drops his mask. With the mask down, you discover a basic inner goodness. You notice this person is driven by the same energies as you are – energies of trying to be his best self, of freedom and of love and belonging. You are drawn to this honest, self-revealing person, in part, because you recognize his core goodness, and you also recognize those same core energies in yourself.

Self-revealing demands courage. Courage means acting from the heart. It implies reaching deep within, listening well to the movements of the heart and responding to those directions openly and honestly. If you believe you're evil or empty at the heart, it becomes more difficult for you to self-reveal than if you like yourself. The risk may seem great, but the results are almost always safe and positive. Self-revelation moves two people closer together.

Begin your self-revealing slowly and easily. Decide beforehand how much you will share. Set your own limits, so you feel in charge of your sharing. It's not helpful to open up "too much," causing you discomfort with the other, especially afterwards. As the relationship grows deeper, you can look for more areas to reveal. The more you and your friend reveal to one another, the deeper the bond between you becomes.

This kind of self-revelation usually demands time and privacy. So arrange times and places for this deeper kind of sharing. While spontaneous, deep sharing can certainly occur, planned sharing at this level requires the environment, space and time that enhances the sharing, and so, the relationship.

Principle 12

**For intimacy to grow, express your *love*
through words as well as actions.**

All marriage counselors have experienced this couple. The wife complains that her husband never tells her he loves her. He snaps back that he's still here, isn't he? He wouldn't still be here if he didn't love her. She, however, would like to hear the words. He says, "Look, I told you I loved you when we got married.

I told you I loved you on our tenth wedding anniversary. And I told you a few years ago. I'll tell you what. Assume I love you. If I change my mind, I'll tell you that."

A boy grows up watching his father acting as the "strong, silent type." He identifies with Dad and, as an adult, keeps everything to himself. He is typical of the man who saw me in therapy for depression. Gary said he never shared any difficulties with his wife because he didn't want her to worry. I asked him if he told her regularly that he loved her. He responded no. I said, "But you are, in fact, loving her each day when you don't talk to her, aren't you? By not wanting her to worry, you are loving her." He understood. "If I love her by protecting her from worry, I might be better off – and she might too – if I told her I loved her. All she sees is me being quiet."

His beliefs about how to love his wife kept him quiet in the relationship. His wife, of course, felt left out and isolated throughout their marriage. Not sharing his concerns and feelings with her was hard enough. Worse yet, she interpreted his silence to mean he didn't care about her and didn't respect her as his partner. And all the while he was loving her by being silent.

A daughter observes her mother being "as tough as nails." This mother gets on with life, never looking back, never pausing for a sensitive, warm moment with her daughter or husband. The mother learned early in her life that she had to protect herself at all times. Talk of love meant hurt, pain and shame.

When she was a child, her father told her how much he loved her and then sexually abused her. She hated it. Whenever he told her he loved her, she froze. She never wanted to hear those words. And she would never invite those words by saying them first to someone else. So she grew up hard on the outside in order to avoid the pain of love. Her daughter, who knew nothing of her mother's history, still learned her mother's behavior. The daughter, however, sought love desperately, for she rarely felt it as a child. But when love came to her, like her mother, she could not return the love in words. She longed to be loved, but never learned how to offer it to another.

Such experiences lead people to feel uncomfortable or unwilling to express love. In the two cases above both people, through therapy, learned what beliefs were controlling their lack of response and worked to improve their verbalness. Many, however, never get in touch with what they learned in childhood and so find it hard to change. These people often say, "Well, that's just the way I am." Such an explanation, of course, implies that they are unable to change. Their inability to express feelings, then, continues the rest of their lives.

Actually, becoming more verbal in expressing love and positive feelings is one of the easier skills to develop. You can start simply and indirectly by bringing the loved one a little gift. Send a card that says in some poetic fashion, "I love you." Then begin saying things like, "I really like you." "It's fun being with you." "I had a good time with you today." From there, it's on to the big time: "Darling, I love you."

If you have trouble expressing loving feelings, talk with your partner, a close friend or a therapist about your beliefs surrounding your lack of expressiveness. Getting in touch with your beliefs gives you the opportunity to change your behavior.

Tell your partner you love her – every day. Don't worry about it becoming routine and losing its meaning. I have yet to meet anyone who tires of hearing those words. Said regularly with feeling and conviction, words of love always touch the heart of the beloved.

Principle 13

**To keep the relationship close,
don't forget to share daily happenings.**

At the beginning of most relationships you make "big talk." You discuss your pasts, your goals, your futures. At some point, you express your limitations to see if the other will accept you. When she does, the relationship accelerates. Such deep conversations make your heart beat faster, but you also find them exhausting. You stay up until 4:00 o'clock in the morning, getting "into each other's lives."

Small talk lightens up the seriousness of getting to know each other. It serves as a break in the intensity of moving toward intimacy. Small talk is like a resting station during a marathon run. It allows you to catch your breath and relax a little. And it offers the needed balance in the movement toward one another.

When you have been together a long time, you may not have as many intense conversations as when you first met. There probably is simply not as much to talk about. You already know a lot about each other. And you learned how to communicate with one another in many non-verbal and intuitive ways. Furthermore, as the relationship grows, you de-focus it. You turn your attention outward, toward careers, children, other interests and friends.

Light chatter is a sign of health in most relationships. A man may be interested in his wife's visit to her mother. A friend asks a friend how his golf game went. A woman asks her boyfriend about the grocery shopping he did. And so on. Small talk includes conversation about everything: the neighbors, sports teams, office workers, the boss, the weather, the book you finished, the television show (certainly soap operas), the brakes on the car. The list goes on.

Over the years I have heard some people, mostly men, say they don't like small talk. It's a waste of time. It bores them. They don't care about the neighbor's kids or the bugs eating the beans in the garden. I have noticed that these people do not engage in serious talk, either. They use the small talk argument as an excuse not to talk at all.

If you are one of these people, please try to get used to small talk. Without it, no words will be spoken between you and your friend. No relationship can be sustained by serious conversation alone. Small talk bonds you. It serves as a bridge between you. Without words your relationship drifts and eventually dies. When you do not use words to connect to the other, the other tends to use even more words to connect to you. Then you can easily complain, "She does enough talking for the both of us. I don't need to say anything." Not fair! Words, no matter how serious or how light, connect people.

So try to remember the little things that happen during the day. At first, just to remind yourself, keep a little notebook. Jot down the simple events of the day. Use the notebook when telling your partner about these happenings.

Try to get enthused about what the other has to say. When she is talking, try to focus on what is being said rather than drifting off into your own thoughts. Small talk is the glue that holds your relationship in place.

Principle 14

**To further deepen your relationship,
you need the skill of understanding.**

If self-revealing bonds you to another, then so does understanding. The very notion of "communication" means to "stand with the unique experience of the other." That's heavy stuff. What happens to your friend is special to her. When you see it, and even feel it from her point of view, it helps her feel cared for and appreciated.

Please don't overestimate your listening skills. Most people, I'm afraid do. They think they are better listeners than they actually are. Take this understanding business seriously. Really attempt to let go – temporarily – of your own view and simply stand with your friend. The result will be greater intimacy between you, with relatively little effort on your part.

For much more on this issue of listening and self-revealing, you should read *Communicating* in this **Life Skills Series**. Here, I just want to identify the need to listen well as essential to achieving intimacy.

Principle 15

**Next to verbal self-revelation, closeness is best
achieved through bodily presence and contact.**

To share your inner life with someone, you use your body as well as your words. You either talk about what is inside of you, or you express yourself in some physical way. Words tend to be more precise. However, touch and physical presence often generate more power.

If you have been at the bedside of a dying person, you know that words seem a weak symbol of your closeness. You hold the dying person's hand, you caress his face. Both of you know what is passing between you. You are there, close and caring.

Many men, in particular, view physical presence as a sign of intimacy. Research has shown that mothers handle baby boys more than they do baby girls under six months of age. Boys learn to make contact through touch and physical presence. A man can be watching television and his wife reading a book in the same room. He can feel close to her in that experience. She also will feel close being quiet in the same room as long as there has been enough verbal exchange going on to help her feel connected. Generally, two people in the same space will feel some closeness. In fact, love has been defined by one writer as "two people occupying the same space."

Normally you encircle yourself with a boundary. You keep most people out. Some you allow in. Others, at times, invade your space. When you accept another's touch, you allow that person into your space. You welcome him into your inner circle. You touch each other's skin but only certain skin – those parts not covered by clothing. In fact, you first usually touch the hand, which has been extended beyond your protective boundaries.

Then, you enter. You touch the other's face or arm. By invitation you come closer. Your face is inches from the other's, and then you touch his cheek with your lips. This person has allowed you to come skin to skin. You have entered very holy ground.

Yet barriers remain. The other is clothed, another boundary protecting even more sacred ground. In passing through that boundary, "by invitation only," your skin touches the other's where few, or perhaps, no other has touched. You feel deep closeness. So close but not complete union. The other is still outside of you. By mutual agreement, you then enter each other's body in the attempt to become one. Intercourse culminates the movement toward intimacy. All the barriers have been taken down. You two have become one.

Once you have touched each other that deeply, you have not just "had sex." You have invited and been invited into one another's inner space. You left yourself open to be joined by another in a union that words have attempted but failed to describe. At this level your bodies have spoken louder than your words.

Physical touch, then, accelerates a relationship, pushing it to further depths of intimacy. Almost any affectionate touch signals a form of commitment which states, "I enter your space with awe and respect and care for all you open up to me. I also open myself to you and trust you too will care for all you find in me." Mean it when you touch someone affectionately. Add words of caring to the touch if you can. And be grateful when the other receives your touch and responds with a touch of his or her own.

Principle 16

**Men and women respond differently
to physical presence.**

Such differences can often cause problems between men and

women. I see these difficulties regularly in marriage counseling. A wife complains about the lack of intimacy in her relationship with her husband. She says, "He never talks with me. He just sits there and watches television or reads the paper." He can't understand what else she wants. He's home every night. He doesn't hang out at bars or with the guys. The two of them are together all the time. He's out cutting the grass. She's near by pulling weeds from the garden. How much closer can two people get? He feels close to her just because she is physically present. For her, simple physical presence is not sufficient. She feels close when they share their feelings and thoughts verbally with one another.

Men and women use their bodies differently in the dance toward intimacy. Men see their bodies as the primary way of connecting to others. Women use words as their main method of contact. Lilian Rubin, in *Intimate Strangers* (Harper & Row, 1983), points out how young boys learned to repress their feelings of warmth toward their mothers (and therefore, in general). They did so to separate from Mom and form an identity different from hers. Yet they still sought bonding with her. So they learned to use the only other tool they could–namely their bodies. They did things with Mom – played physical games, hugged her, hit her, ran around her, annoyed her. Girls, on the other hand, remained connected to Mom and identified with her. They did not repress their feelings and learned to express them verbally. They learned the way to connect was by expressing feelings through words.

Women need to grow in their comfort with men's approach to closeness, while men need to become comfortable with women's approach. A woman told me she sat for two hours recently with the man she loved, snuggled in his arms without uttering a word. The physical contact was not sexual. It was simply a matter of two people feeling intimate through their bodies. At that moment this woman felt comfortable with physical presence, without words. In a good relationship the man, at some other time, would need to feel equally comfortable with words and no physical contact.

When a man and woman marry, they usually have already attained some level of mutual comfort using words and bodily presence as modes of reaching intimacy. But as the relationship develops, other factors tend to interfere with the couples' ability to maintain physical presence. Careers carry the man and/or woman away from the other. A friend explained to me how his wife is on the road at least three days a week. It allows little time together. Occasionally, married sports figures will announce retirements early because they want to spend more time with their families.

Another obstacle to physical presence is children. Most parents have the experience of my wife and me. Often these days we find ourselves waving to each other in our cars as we pass one another carting children in opposite directions to their events. Children demand our attention and time. It becomes a creative effort to try finding time for our marriage partner. That's why counselors the world over tell couples to take time for themselves, to go away for a weekend or to get out together once a week.

Being physical with your partner and doing things together both help a couple maintain its intimacy. When you link physical presence with verbal communication, you have an unbeatable combination.

Principle 17

Be sensitive to your own and your partner's physical needs, especially for space and time.

You appreciate some time alone. While you move toward union with others, you also value the breathing space that "alone time" offers. In all your relationships, you need to be sensitive to your own need for space and time as well as the other's need.

Space and time help you define yourself, allowing you to

recognize who you are and what's going on inside of you. Alone time actually helps you relate more effectively to your partner because you become more aware of your thoughts and feelings. You can only share what you are aware of.

Alone time also gives you a chance to get filled up. You spend the majority of your life at work and at home giving to others. You need a chance to receive, to refresh yourself. Spending quiet time reading, thinking, walking or working on a hobby are all ways of restoring yourself so you can continue giving at work and to your family.

Finally, alone time increases your awareness of the world around you as well as your inner world. Whenever you get reflective, you become more tuned in to life. On your walk you notice the hectic pace you have been keeping, the physical strain that has been sapping your energy, the brightness of the stars tonight, the soft cool breeze of the evening wind, the quiet of the neighborhood. Or as you read the biography that speaks to your heart, you understand how another person lived, how another culture affected its people, why a war happened and how a father influenced his son. Alone time broadens your mental and emotional horizons.

Gaining a balance between time alone and time with another can be difficult. It demands sensitivity to your own needs as well as the other's. If you know your partner needs some time, you can help him arrange it. You can pick up the slack to make it possible for him to gain what he needs. In fact, partners that work well together tend to encourage each other to take time. Such encouragement works only if each person feels the other is being sensitive to his or her needs as well.

Ginny strongly resisted her husband, Bob, taking time alone after supper to work in the garden while she had to clean up, take care of the kids and do the wash. Later in the evening when she wanted to sit and talk with him, he was glued to the television set. She resented him taking time for himself to play with this garden hobby. Had he washed the dishes and cleaned the kitchen; had he sat with her later in the evening talking about the day, Ginny would not have be-grudged him taking time to weed the garden. In fact, she would have encouraged him to do so.

You will be glad to give alone time to your partner if your partner meets your needs as well. Creating a rhythm of time together and time alone strengthens your relationship and makes the time you spend with each other much more interesting, stimulating and intimate.

Principle 18

Keep the attraction alive in your relationship.

Throughout the span of a special relationship, you need to feel a *draw* toward each other. Without that attraction, the relationship loses its spark. Another word for draw is passion.

You keep the draw alive in several ways. The first is to develop common interests. Perhaps you both enjoy similar things – music, art, sports. You're lucky if you find common ground without having to work at it. You clicked because you started out with interests that matched.

But many times, as a relationship goes on, you need to *work* at creating common interests. You must stretch your limits, try to open yourself to your partner's directions. It's as if you're learning a new language or culture. It feels strange and unknown. But you choose to enter the different and foreign world of your friend's interests.

Emotional involvement in mutual goals or projects also helps draw a relationship. Two attorneys, one a man, the other a woman, work on the same case for months. They go to court and win the case. Working together to accomplish a specific job, plus the shared emotional high of successfully reaching a goal, draws the two together. They fall in love, despite each being married to another. The "office romance" comes alive.

Two people working on a common goal generally experience some kind of attraction and warmth toward each other. They need not fall in love as our attorneys did, but they will feel good about each other and closer to one another.

Another source of attraction lies in the *emotion* of an event. You go to the opera with your friend. The experience is filled with drama, passion and intensity. You are filled with emotion by the happening. You share that emotion with each other. You are drawn together.

As the relationship goes on, however, other priorities and distractions can interfere. Perhaps you start wandering down one path and your partner down another. You drift. You become pre-occupied with your own world and slowly lose track of each other.

While "drifting" can easily occur in a committed relationship, it need not. Creating common goals and directions brings you back toward each other. If you are married and have children, common goals can and need to be developed and pursued around the following issues:

1. Finances.
2. Child-rearing practices.
3. Careers.
4. Maintaining home and property.
5. Vacations and leisure.
6. Personal growth needs.
7. Physical care: exercise, diet and health.
8. Children's educational needs.
9. Retirement planning.
10. Common work projects on the job or at home.
11. Spiritual growth.
12. Extended family relationships.
13. Developing adult and couple friendships.
14. Sexual relationship.

All of these goals carry emotional overtones with them. Accomplishing the goals through a cooperative effort draws you more powerfully to each other and gives you the feeling of truly having a *partner*. You share the dream, the struggle to reach the dream, the joy of grasping it or the sorrow of losing it.

Principle 19

**Strive for mutuality rather than a
one-up/one-down relationship.**

You are born into a relationship where you are one-down. For the first years of your life you know only one-down. Totally dependent, you look to your all-powerful parents for everything from food to love. You desperately need them. But you don't like your position. One-down feels scary, demeaning and insecure. So you attempt to rise up. Since all you know is the opposite of one-down, you attempt to go one-up to your parents.

Early in life you learn your strategies. You cry until they respond. You push things off the table you don't like. Later on, you employ the powerful word "No!" A baby brother comes along and you delight in playing one-up to him.

The story of your early life centers on one-up/one-down dynamics. Off you go to kindergarten. You feel one-down. You try going one-up to the teacher. You work your way to the top of elementary school, fifth grade. You are one-up. Then you proceed to middle school and find yourself one-down. You get to the eighth grade and once again you are one-up. You enter high school and go one down. So it goes throughout your schooling. You finally graduate on top of the academic world, only to go one-down in the work world. Throughout your work career you struggle, going one-up to one-down back to one-up.

Your life experiences taught you well how to navigate these one-up/one-down relationships. Someplace in your early teen years, however, you had a different experience. You entered a relationship that did not seem to show the power dynamic of one-up/one-down. It felt mutual or equal. You didn't compete. You didn't attempt to dominate the other. It felt strange, but good. You began the journey toward a rewarding type of relationship, one characterized by *mutuality* rather than one-up/one-down power.

Relationships can be pocketed into two large categories: *mutual* and *unequal*. Friendships, adult family relationships, marriages and co-workers at the same level in the work force are examples of mutual relationships. Employer-employee, therapist-client, teacher-student, parent-child and coach-player are examples of unequal power relationships. Due to your long experience with unequal power relationships, many one-up/one-down dynamics tend to spill over into your mutual relationships. Furthermore, our culture penetrates mutual relationships with heavy beliefs that reinforce the one-up/one-down model of relating.

Studies on marriage report that men traditionally have more power than women. This seems to occur, in part, because men are physically larger and can employ brute force to get their way. Generally they have more educational opportunities and more employment possibilities, giving them greater income, social status and expertise.

Not only do husbands make more decisions than wives, but those with more income and social status possess more power in their marriages than husbands with less income and status. All this points to the difficulty in maintaining mutuality in significant relationships.

Whoever possesses the greatest *power* seems to determine the balance or equality of the relationship. Relational power arises from holding what the other needs. If the mother possesses the milk the baby needs, mother has the power. If the boss holds the job security the laborer seeks, the boss has the power. If the husband keeps the affirmation the wife craves, the husband has the power.

Anne Campbell, in her book, *The Opposite Sex*, (Salem House

Pub., 1989) states it well: "My power over someone else depends upon our relative dependence on each other. If we each have something the other wants, and are equally dependent on each other, then neither has the power advantage. But if one person is more dependent, that gives the other person more power."

For instance, if you are more emotionally involved in the relationship than the other, you will be more dependent and have less power. If you seek more closeness and want more intimate communication than your husband, you become dependent on him, giving him more power. Thus, both of you enhance the mutuality of the relationship by needing one another in generally equal amounts. Mutual dependence promotes mutuality.

Couples strive to balance one another's power in the relationship. As indicated above, men still tend to play a more one-up position in heterosexual relationships. They tend also to express their power more directly than women. They exert physical force, issue commands rather than consult, wield their expertise or knowledge. Men tend to talk to, ask or tell their wives directly what they want.

In order to balance this *overt* power exercised by men, women often employ *covert* power styles. They tend to use indirect forms of exerting power, such as helplessness or pleas for affection. Women attempt to influence men in more indirect ways, such as pretending to be nice, hinting or pouting. In these less obvious ways, then, they attempt to balance their male partner's overt power.

Balancing power through overt-covert methods does not enhance intimacy in a relationship. Employing any power strategies, whether they be overt or covert, keeps the couple in a competitive rather than cooperative relationship. As long as you focus on ways to "stay on top" or "get up from the bottom" you will miss the enriching experience of mutuality.

Mutuality occurs only when both of you recognize your needs for each other and rely on one another to fulfill those needs. Intimacy takes place when you open yourselves to each other verbally and physically, knowing you can trust in the loving response of the other person. Then you are safe in each other's presence. You are valued and loved by one another. You know fulfillment in the embrace of the one you love most.

Chapter Three

Developing this Skill with Others

It may feel redundant to talk about developing the skill of intimacy by working with others. But in this brief section I want to encourage you to *work* at increasing intimacy by consciously reflecting and practicing the skill with a partner or a group.

The following steps are suggested:

Step 1

Use this book as a basis for discussion. You can take one principle or tool at a time, read it and discuss its application to your own life. The more personal you make the discussion the better.

Step 2

Try to determine your level of *comfort* in relationships. How much intimacy do you like? When do you start feeling anxious in a relationship? When do you feel too distant? Try to assess your intimate partner's comfort with intimacy as well.

Step 3

Try to determine what you *need* and what you *want* in your close relationships. See if you have expressed those needs to your partner. If not, get to it. If you have, then consider how you might do it again in a way he or she can better hear you.

Step 4

Ask your intimate partner what his or her needs are, and whether he or she feels you are meeting them. Come back to your discussion person or group and share what you have learned about your needs and your partner's needs.

Step 5

Encourage others in the group to take risks in their relationships by being self-revealing. If one of you attempts to be self-revealing in an intimate relationship at home and your partner doesn't pay attention to you, let the person know she can return to the group for your support and empathy. Use the group as your security blanket.

Conclusion

Achieving intimacy in this life stands as one of your greatest accomplishments. Its rewards far outweigh its risks. Although many relationships end up on the trash heap of love, your ability to avoid such a trial will be determined by how hard you work at this skill. You can learn to be intimate. You can minimize the chances that your special relationships will fail. By conscious effort to move *toward* intimacy rather than away from it, to listen well to your partner and to self-reveal, you will find the joy, peace and union that intimacy provides.

Appendix

Review of Principles for Being Intimate

1. Try to move toward people rather than away from them.
2. Develop clear personal boundaries between you and the other person.
3. Create positive labels to allow the relationship to grow more fully.
4. Keep the other person a top priority.
5. Work to love the *real* other and not the *ideal* other.
6. Accept the other for better and for worse.
7. Develop an attitude of flexibility.
8. Be ready and willing to forgive and be forgiven.
9. Understand that your emotional responses decrease over time as your intimacy increases.
10. To reach a deep level of intimacy, you need to reveal yourself through verbal communication.
11. The more you self-reveal, the more the other person bonds to you.

12. For intimacy to grow, express your *love* through words as well as actions.
13. To keep the relationship close, don't forget to share daily happenings.
14. To further deepen your relationship, you need the skill of understanding.
15. Next to verbal self-revelation, closeness is best achieved through bodily presence and contact.
16. Men and women respond differently to physical presence.
17. Be sensitive to your own and your partner's physical needs, especially for space and time.
18. Keep the attraction alive in your relationship.
19. Strive for mutuality rather than a one-up/one-down relationship.